QUIET CORNERS OF ROME

Quiet Corners of

BY DAVID DOWNIE

PHOTOGRAPHS BY ALISON HARRIS

THE LITTLE BOOKROOM ◆ NEW YORK

We would like to give warmest thanks to Carla Bertini, Verdella Caracciolo, Angela Hederman,
Patrizia Masini, and Claudio and Claudia Volpetti.

Library of Congress Cataloging-in-Publication Data

Downie, David.
Quiet corners of Rome / by David Downie ; photographs by Alison Harris.
p. cm.
Includes index.
ISBN 1-892145-92-8 (alk. paper)
1. Rome (Italy)--Guidebooks. 2. Rome (Italy)--Description and travel. I. Title.
DG804.D69 2010
914.5'6320493--dc22
2010026820

Printed in the United States of America

Published by The Little Bookroom
435 Hudson Street, Suite 300
New York NY 10014
editorial@littlebookroom.com
www.littlebookroom.com

2 4 6 8 0 9 7 5 3 1

Contents

Foreword

⟞∽⟐∽⟼

The boughs of an umbrella pine sway in the breeze as swallows swoop high above your head. Over the tiled rooftops church bells toll at a sleepy distance. But nothing can cover the mesmerizing play of the rococo fountain whose cool water is tickling your feet. It's hard to believe you're no longer lounging in the campagna or that the chaotic capital of Italy spreads below. Rome? There are no quiet corners in Rome!

You're right to be skeptical. Rome, the Eternal City, is endlessly fascinating, lovable, lively—and loud. No matter how many eternal clichés are thrown at it, the one unspinnable fact is Rome and silence are foes. "The smoke, the wealth, the noise of Rome!" cried Horace. That was two thousand years ago. Multiply by degrees of magnitude, add in Vespas, sirens and megaphones, and you can just hear grumpy Horace repeating his other famous line, "I hate the vulgar crowd, and keep them away: grant me your silence!"

Lucky fellow! He had a divine muse, a fervent imagination and powerful backers. Horace also spent most of his time in suburban villas, living the life of a patrician. Wealthy Romans still decamp whenever they can to family estates far from the madding crowd. But how do other contemporary natives—and the thirty-nine million visitors to Rome each year—

deal with the nonstop animation? Easy: either they learn to tune out the background noise, or know where to escape it.

Happily, in Rome, searching for quiet corners is a treasure hunt. You find not only the far-flung and unsung, but also the occasional hidden gem glinting amid the bustling throngs.

That treasure hunt includes the masterpieces of art and architecture lurking around every corner—and sometimes perched several stories up a faded façade. Parks spread behind high walls. Echoing courtyards lie at the end of tangled alleyways. But how to find them?

The modest mission of this book, assembled after years of exploration, is to show that when in Rome, you really can do as the Romans do and make the city's secrets your own. For a starter, the nine hundred–odd churches salted among the Seven Hills are guaranteed sanctuaries. Nearly all harbor inner courts, cloisters or crypts where quiet is the operative word—and no photography is allowed. A few are included here. The others are obvious.

If you're seeking tranquility that includes the great outdoors, or a nonreligious setting, you need to look elsewhere. You have to take the long way around, the back street, the unexpected turning in the alley in the neighborhood you would not normally visit—the Piccolo Aventino, for instance, or Garbatella and Monteverde. Never heard of them? That's a good thing. You'll be all the more surprised and, it's hoped, delighted, when you stumble upon that splashing fountain, those swaying pines, and that sensation of quietude you thought you'd never experience in wonderful old noisy Rome.

GHETTO, CAMPO DE' FIORI, TIBER ISLAND, PANTHEON, PIAZZA NAVONA

——ഗ∕ഗ——

Vicolo Costaguti

GHETTO

Entrances: Via del Portico d'Ottavia, Piazza Costaguti, Vicolo Costaguti
Metro: n/a
Open daily

✦

Several shrines—either temples of gastronomy or faith—crowd along the Ghetto's main street, Via del Portico d'Ottavia, and the alleyways that branch off it. Recently pedestrianized on its western end, the Ghetto has become a stroller's and cyclist's paradise. Balconies jut from patchwork palazzi of uncertain age—meaning they were built at some point between antiquity and a century or three ago. Finding the cave-like Vicolo Costaguti and the secret courtyard it reveals can be a challenge.

Start by asking anyone for Boccioni, the celebrated pastry shop. Once you've bought your ricotta cake, step out, turn right, and you'll find yourself facing an unusual shrine. It's unusual for several reasons: colonnaded and semi-circular, with a Latin inscription, it looks like a cage, closed off by tall iron bars. In the center of the cage a work of contemporary art often stands.

Flanking the shrine to the left is an archway. It leads under a palazzo painted burnt sienna, through a cavernous, low, dark passageway—the elusive Vicolo Costaguti—into a courtyard the size of a modest living room. Green plants—ferns, yuccas and potted loquats arranged by locals into a haphazard circle—serve as a centerpiece for this hideaway. On the stoops of surrounding buildings you'll probably see residents and school kids sitting in the pleasant obscurity, chilling out, snacking and chatting sotto voce. This is one of the ancient Jewish neighborhood's least known, semi-enclosed *salotti*—public salons that feel cozy and private. Shhhh, don't tell anyone.

Theater of Marcellus, Via del Portico d'Ottavia

GHETTO

Entrances: Via del Portico d'Ottavia, Via di Sant'Angelo in Pescheria, Via del Foro Piscario
Metro: n/a
Open daily, sunrise to sunset

◆

The Via del Portico d'Ottavia is the Ghetto's main street. Where it curves as it nears the Tiber, a row of broken columns—the remains of Octavia's Portico—push up from the sidewalk like dinosaur bones. Among them, look for the tables of trattoria Giggetto, often piled with artichokes. Next door is the jumbled front of a Romanesque church,

Sant'Angelo in Pescheria. Another fifty feet southeast rises the Theater of Marcellus, a looming, snaggletooth pile in an archeological park, topped since the 1930s by the sumptuous apartments of the rich and famous. A ramp leads down into the park. As you pick your way through the toppled capitals and mounds of sculpted marble, it's worth remembering that Augustus Caesar rebuilt the portico from the second century BC and dedicated it to his sister, Octavia. The theater, started by Julius Caesar, also inherited by Augustus, bears the name of his nephew, Marcellus. In the Middle Ages it became the fortress-residence of the Orsini clan. Their Tiber-side entrance, still used, is strictly off limits to mere mortals.

Climb back out of the ruins and onto the short bridge over the excavations. If you stop halfway, you'll have the best view of the theater, portico and church. Frescoes on the façade, bleached by sunshine, depict a winged angel. The house-plants of neighbors lean from windowsills and terraces. Relatively modern, eighth-century Sant'Angelo in Pescheria housed Rome's main fish market, the Foro Piscario (or Pescheria), for seven hundred years. On the archway by the main door, a plaque evokes the privilege of Rome's municipal magistrates, who were given the heads of prized fish, a delicacy back then. Relax on the shady bench nearby. You might just feel you're part of a Piranesi print. Luckily, the fishy smell vanished a century ago.

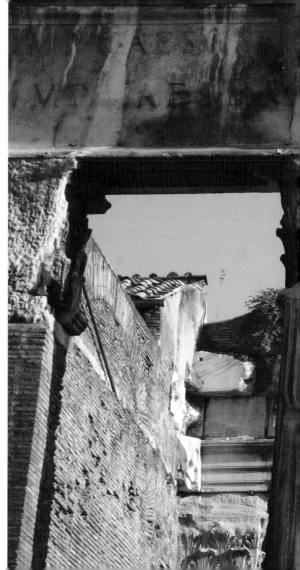

Palazzo Mattei di Giove

—◈—

GHETTO
Entrance: Via Michelangelo Caetani 32
Metro: n/a
Open Monday–Thursday 10am–6pm, Friday 10am–2pm
Tel: 06 688 01613, www.centrostudiamericani.org

◆

If you've ever wondered what happened to all those ancient sculptures and architectural details dug up in Rome during the Renaissance, step through the cavernous entrance to Palazzo Mattei di Giove, a hulking brick townhouse whose rusticated corners mark the edge of the Ghetto. You may just have an epiphany. Sticking out of the high walls of the palazzo's double courtyards or mounted on pedestals, is a Whitman's Sampler of archaeology. Slightly sinister, there's a monumental mask long used as a fountain spout, a marble sarcophagus with chipped lion heads, reliefs showing bulls and beasts, and dozens of busts or full-size statues, some headless, of heroes, athletes and emperors. Not only did the architects and antiquarians of the 1500s and 1600s plunder the sites of their ancient forebears, they also added missing parts, or resculpted the artworks of old, to fit the décor of the luxurious palaces they built for wealthy patrons.

One of the greatest showcases for this kind of fashionable looting is this palazzo, built by Carlo Maderno between 1598 and 1617, for the plutocratic Mattei clan, owners of the village of Giove, near Terni, in Umbria. The Mattei's palaces and squares in Rome are many. One of the city's most beloved fountains—la Fontana delle Tartarughe—rises fifty yards away, in Piazza Mattei.

Poke around the echoing courtyards of Palazzo Mattei di Giove, wander up the imposing staircase, and glance around from the loggia. Certainly, the art and architecture are glorious. What you might appreciate even more is the magical atmosphere. Heels click on marble. The custodian's broom sweeps at the cobbles. Voices and music well up from unseen recesses. Professors, writers, artists and curators come and go, talking not only of Michelangelo, but also of the many cross-cultural topics that bind Italy and America. Since 1936, the property has housed the Centro di Studi Americani, a nonprofit institution where historians, politicians, essayists, novelists and actors hold conferences or study.

Arco degli Acetari

CAMPO DE' FIORI
Entrance: Via del Pellegrino 19
Metro: n/a
Open daily

◆

Sunwashed Pompeii meets burnt sienna—as in rustic, rusty red and earthy orange—in the plastered brick and stonework of this cobbled medieval courtyard, hidden down an arcaded alley off Via del Pellegrino, about 150 feet west of Campo de' Fiori. Rome's vinegar-makers—*gli acetari*—had their workshops here long ago. On the wheel-worn fluted columns protruding from scraped walls you can see the abrasive tracework made by countless vinegar

carts trundling to and fro. But where souring wine once reposed, nowadays you'll find a peaceful, laundry-strung urban jungle with a distinctively arty feel. Grapevines clothe the higgledy-piggledy building whose cliff-face leans over the entrance. Perfumed pittosporum shrubs vie with tangled wisteria, while miniature yuccas and cactuses fill pots on balconies and curving outdoor stairways. In the middle of the courtyard, bicycles huddle for protection from Rome's celebrated bicycle thieves. One battered old three-wheeler has been converted into a plant stand. Of course there are motor scooters too. And a barbecue in one corner, a hint that life here is sometimes a block party.

Several residents offer short-term apartment rentals in buildings on the courtyard, and an art gallery at #40 sells a mixed bag of contemporary creativity. You'll rarely feel crowded here, in fact you'll almost certainly be alone. Felines outnumber humans, and come in a kaleidoscope of colors. Happily in this fortunate enclave black cats don't seem to bring bad luck. Who knows, they may even have the opposite effect, adding to the be-witching calm.

Arco di Santa Margherita

———⟨ formatting ornament ⟩———

CAMPO DE' FIORI
Entrances: Via del Pellegrino 15, Via dei Cappellari 35
Metro: n/a
Open daily

✦

A few doors down Via del Pellegrino from Arco degli Acetari, another atmospheric alleyway awaits you. You'll have no trouble spotting the entrance to Arco di Santa Margherita. One of Rome's most elaborate street-corner shrines is affixed to the second floor. Its wings splayed out and its back arched in the style of a caryatid, an eagle props up the Madonna, airborne cupids poised above her. There's a trompe-l'oeil window to the right. Laundry flutters from railings. A water fountain splashes below, providing the background music. Don't be put off by the graffiti or gloom. The alleyway does a dog's leg, burrowing under medieval buildings, with stone columns and thresholds. In the shadows cower the carts of the greengrocers from Campo de' Fiori, parked here when not in use, a centuries-old tradition. Follow the alley to its end at Via dei Cappellari, another medieval byway not much wider than Arco di Santa Margherita. Where Rome's hatters once worked, nowadays you'll find artists' studios, galleries and antiques shops—plus nightclubs, bars and restaurants. Few places in town are more lively at midnight—or quieter in the morning and afternoon.

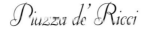

Piazza de' Ricci

CAMPO DE' FIORI

Entrances: Via di Monserrato, Via Giulia, Via di Sant'Aurea
Metro: n/a
Open daily

✦

In hot weather, when the handsomely dressed tables at landmark Ristorante Pierluigi are full to capacity, and every window on the compact square is thrown open, Piazza de' Ricci is not exactly quiet, though it never gets as noisy as nearby Campo de' Fiori or Piazza Farnese. Much of the rest of the time tranquility reigns: sometimes you can even hear the sound of asparagus ferns swaying from the lavishly bearded balcony on Via di Monserrato overlooking the square. Emanating from the interior of massive Palazzo Ricci dance the notes of virtuoso restorers at work, testing and tuning the musical instruments left in their care. Get closer, so you can peer up through the heavy iron bars and windows. Violins, violas, cellos and other stringed instruments hang like so many *prosciutti* from the rafters of a workshop, on the corner of the piazza and Via di Sant'Aurea. That's what the alley that links Piazza de' Ricci to straight, quintessentially Renaissance Via Giulia is called. Raise your eyes and directly above the workshop you'll spot a hovering, garlanded shrine to the Madonna, held aloft by the kind of putto seen in better postcards. The noble, sixteenth-century palazzo for which the square is named stands out among neighboring buildings for its rusticated corners, yellowish brickwork and the faded frescoes on the façade between the ground and first floors.

Piazza della Quercia

-∾∾∾-

CAMPO DE' FIORI

Entrances: Vicolo del Polverone, Via di Capo di Ferro, Via dei Balestrari
Metro: n/a
Open daily

✦

Can't locate Piazza della Quercia? It's shaded by the old ilex—a holm oak, if you prefer—that gave its name to the tennis court-sized oasis fronting Palazzo Spada. A rotund Baroque church, Santa Maria della Quercia, hides its pistachio-hued head in one corner, but is often closed. Few notice it as they march from Michelangelo's façade, appended to nearby Palazzo Farnese, into the museum housed by the neighborhood's other Renaissance jewel, Palazzo Spada. By all means, visit the museum. Once you've feasted upon the courtyard and architectural perspectives by Borromini and Bernini, the artworks by Reni, Rubens, Andrea del Sarto and Dürer, rest your eyes in this pleasant *piazzetta*, where the tables of a trattoria spread.

Isola Tiberina

TIBER ISLAND

Entrances: Ponte Cestio, Ponte Fabricio
Metro: n/a
Open daily

◆

Ship-shaped and battered by an incessant flow of water, the small, rocky island in the middle of the Tiber is a favorite haunt among Romans for jogging, strolling, sunbathing and picnicking. At water-level there's always a breeze. The roar of the river tumbling over dams and stone pilings covers other sounds, giving a new spin to the concept of deafening silence. Much of the upstream end of Isola Tiberina is occupied by Fatebenefratelli hospital, while the downstream end hosts the church of San Bartolomeo all'Isola (and a police station). Under the

church lies a buried temple to Aesculapius, the ancient Greek god of medicine. His effigy was brought to plague-ridden Rome by ship up the Tiber in 291 BC. A serpent slid away from the convoy and slithered onto the island, clearly expressing the god's will. Isola Tiberina was promptly reconfigured to resemble the ship, and upon it the temple rose (and the medical profession got its symbol, a snake twined around a staff). Or so the legend goes.

Since the 1700s Rome's neoclassical Temple to Aesculapius has stood on the lakeside in Villa Borghese.

Nowadays the best way to reach the island's marble-paved quays is via a staircase near the ambulance entrance to the hospital. Look for the pine trees, climb down the stairs and through an iron gate, then double back to the downstream tip. A cool, leafy corner on this otherwise sunwashed island, it's shaded by towering sycamores whose knotted roots cling to the cracked stonework. Close-up views feature the crumbled Ponte Rotto—Rome's celebrated "broken bridge." Only one span stands, the others having collapsed into the Tiber's waves in 1598.

Piazza della Pigna

PANTHEON

Entrances: Via della Pigna, Vicolo delle Ceste, Vicolo della Minerva, Via del Gesù
Metro: n/a
Open daily

✦

Recently pedestrianized on its western end, the pretty little piazza fronting the church of San Giovanni della Pigna, and the alleys leading to it, are a quiet, colorful corner in one of Rome's oldest, most densely touristed neighborhoods. All the classic colors of the city meet, from russet and brick, to peach, apricot and orange, or faded Pompeii red. After the gigantism and wildly Baroque decoration of the Church of Il Gesù, a few hundred yards south, the plain pilasters, composite capitals and mossy tile roof of San Giovanni della Pigna come as a relief. Not one but two hovering Madonnas gaze out from street-corner shrines.

Food is part of the equation: a likable trattoria, named for the square, spreads its tables across this compact refuge. But what of the *pigna*—the ancient bronze pine cone that gave the square, street and district their name? The pagans of Rome revered it as a symbol of eternal life. Naturally, in the enlightened Middle Ages, the subversive object was removed to the Vatican—for safe keeping. From the church, walk down Vicolo delle Ceste, do an about-face and look up carefully at what crowns the pilasters on the side of San Giovanni della Pigna: the pine cone lives on, in the form of a modest bas relief.

Via della Pace

PIAZZA NAVONA

Entrances: Via della Pace, Vicolo della Pace
Metro: n/a
Open daily

◆

Peace Street? That's what the name means. The crowded cafés of Rome's vociferous hipsters stand shoulder-to-shoulder on the southern end of Via della Pace. But the northern end of this cobbled street just one hundred yards west of Piazza Navona becomes a bagpipe-shaped bulge facing the extraordinary church of Santa Maria della Pace.

What's so extraordinary? Santa Maria della Pace is the quintessence of the Renaissance, built in the 1480s, but has a peculiar octagonal nave with a coffered ceiling, and its façade is convex. Inside are frescoes by Raphael and Peruzzi. Flanking the church is another extraordinary piece of architecture: Bramante's cloister, from 1504. It proves that sobriety can be stunning. What Bramante would think of the cloister's upper-level café, with comfy, cushioned seats and silken cappuccinos served where ascetics once paced, is an open question.

Back on the street, the exterior embellishments of the *piazzetta* are effusively Baroque, signed Pietro da Cortona. How could he have guessed that Rome would one day be overrun by motor vehicles? Serendipitously, with an eye to aesthetics and balance, the masterful architect-artist added the semicircular portico in 1656, flanked by symmetrical passageways that thwart traffic to this day.

CAPITOLINE (CAMPIDOGLIO), VELABRUM, FORUM, PALATINE

M · D · LXXXIIII

Piazzale Caffarelli

CAMPIDOGLIO

Entrances: Via del Teatro di Marcello, Via delle Tre Pile, La Cordonata, Piazza d'Aracoeli,
Piazza del Campidoglio, Rampa Caffarelli
Metro: Colosseo
Open daily

◆

As you head toward Piazzale Caffarelli from Michelangelo's architectural masterpiece—the trapezoidal Piazza del Campidoglio, fronting city hall—and pass under a monumental gateway built in 1584, count your paces. Depending on your stride, you probably won't top a hundred by the time you've walked up the last stretch of coiling Via delle Tre Pile, away from the gathered thousands, and find yourself on a panoramic garden terrace perched high above Via del Teatro di Marcello. Chaos abates, then almost disappears. Catch your breath and get used to being alone. The views cover at least 180 degrees and thirty-five centuries of historic gorgeousness. They reach from the Tiber and the Ghetto to Piazza Venezia and, of course, the famous Cordonata staircase tilting up in stony bands from Piazza d'Aracoeli to city hall, as if it had been designed for horses, not humans. From this perspective, the stern church of the Aracoeli looks like an Incan Temple, and the winged sculptures on the glaringly white Vittoriano—"The Typewriter" to Romans—seem downright graceful.

Pedestrians are dwarfed by the outsized, ancient statues of Castor and Pollux that guard the summit of the staircase and the spectacular, wisteria-draped pergola parallel to it.

The terrace at Piazzale Caffarelli occupies what was the top floor of the partly demolished Caffarelli family palace, built in the 1500s and finished a century later. But underneath the site lie Bronze Age settlements going back 1,500 years before the Christian Era, not to mention multiple layers of early Rome. The terrace, planted with ilex trees and lined by cool, travertine benches, has been a public park for a bat of the Roman eye, i.e., since 1918.

Scala dell'Arce Capitolina

CAMPIDOGLIO

Entrances: Piazza del Campidoglio, Via di San Pietro in Carcere
Metro: Colosseo
Open daily

◆

Standing on the brick-and-stone staircase known as the Scala dell'Arce Capitolina, you'd never guess that Caput Mundi—the "head of the world" and center of the Roman universe—lies only a hundred feet away, centered below on the gilded bronze equestrian statue of Marcus Aurelius in the Piazza del Campidoglio. Once you've admired the dizzyingly magnificent scene—the décor is signed Michelangelo—turn toward the Forum, leave the crowds behind, and walk up the staircase, following the unobtrusive little sign pointing to the Aracoeli.

Steep enough to discourage most visitors, the staircase, made of multiple, gentle flights, lies atop the ancient path to early Rome's great citadel, the Arx. It's now the quiet back way into the Aracoeli, the brick-built medieval church, and also gives access to the terraces of the glaringly white Vittoriano, the so-called "Temple of the *Patria*" that pushes up against the Capitoline Hill.

Twenty-six centuries ago, back in the days of Tarquin the Elder, when they dug up the skull—the *caput*—that gave the Capitoline its name, did the Romans have any sense of the antiquity of the site, or what it would become? Bronze-age huts stood here long before the Romans' temples of Jupiter or Veiovis. The temples are still around, buried now, by too many layers to describe. What's most amazing, though, is that you can feel so impossibly light-hearted treading on top of it all.

When you reach the column crowned by a ball and a cross, halfway up the staircase, turn left, climb another dozen steps, and lean on the balustrade of the hidden *piazzetta*. Stand still long enough and imagine the wings of the Vittoriano's "Winged Victory" sprouting on your back. Before your eyes on the eastern horizon is the Palatine, the Forum below it, and, in the foreground, one side of city hall, encrusted with marble tablets and commemorative reliefs. Swarmed by tour groups, the She-Wolf of Rome glares down from atop her column. If you tire of solitude, at the base of the staircase there's a small park. Few seem to spot its gravel lanes and benches, from which you'll enjoy many of the same views, offered from a slightly lower altitude.

Via del Tempio di Giove and Piazzetta di Monte Caprino

CAMPIDOGLIO

Entrances: Via di Monte Caprino, Via del Tempio di Giove, Vico Jugario
Metro: Colosseo
Open daily

◆

The Temple of Jupiter is no longer above ground—it's underneath the Renaissance buildings of the Capitoline Museum, and features in the displays. But the looping lane called Via del Tempio di Giove that once led to it still crosses the crest and girds the southwestern slope of this most ancient of Rome's hills. The lane turns into a staircase that lowers intrepid explorers to a tiny *piazzetta* and a garden alleyway called Via di Monte Caprino. There are no goatherds to be seen, though they used this cobbled ramp until recently—a century or so ago. Back then, the Forum was called "the cow pasture," and this side of the Capitoline was "goat mountain."

Today, majestic towering pines and low-lying leafy trees hide the square from prying eyes. The views over the Theater of Marcellus may not be as dramatic as they are from the top of the hill. But the secret, shady quality of the spot makes it perfect for a romantic tryst, or a quiet rest before you face the crowds. From here, landscaped staircases lead down to Vico Jugario and the back entrance to the Forum.

Arco di Giano

VELABRUM

Entrances: Via del Velabro, Via di San Giovanni Decollato, Via di San Teodoro
Metro: Circo Massimo
Open daily

◆

Perhaps fate decreed that the Velabrum be a backwater. It was, literally, about 2,800 years ago and it is, metaphorically, today. Legend has it that this once swampy area between the Forum and the Tiber is where the roots of a fig tree snagged the floating basket in which babies Romulus and Remus were delivered, providentially, to the site of the city they were soon to found. The Velabrum lived its heyday millennia ago, but subsided into quietude in the early 1900s. Since then, the mainstream of cars, buses and foot traffic has flowed noisily along the Tiber-side expressways, and through Piazza Bocca della Verità, where the Temples of Portunus and Hercules Victor stand, and the church of Santa Maria in Cosmedin offers its voracious "mouth of truth" to countless hands.

Just one hundred yards north, away from the bustle, the Velabrum begins. In Republican Rome it became the crossroads linking the Forum to the riverside cattle market, and the Capitoline to the Palatine. Today its focal point is the Arco di Giano—the Arch of Janus. Squat and muscular, its four arches make this gateway one of a kind. In the Middle Ages they also gave it a misleading

name: Janus was the god of thresholds, but this was never his four-fronted temple.

Recent by Roman standards, the arch was built in the fourth century AD, probably in honor of Emperor Constantine. But war, wear and weathering have taken their toll. Seemingly made of melting marble, a kind of geological marvel, the archway's niches stand empty, lavishly sculpted with upside-down conch shells, a decorative motif reprised time and again by pagans and Christians. Restored recently, fenced in by ironwork, and surrounded by a cobbled piazza dotted with benches, the archway and its surroundings are now an island of peace. If you can't get into the cobbled piazza—it's sometimes locked when it should be open—don't lose heart. A stairway from the Velabrum to Via di San Giovanni Decollato provides a perch. The road from the Arco di Giano—Via del Velabro—to Via di San Teodoro is also car-free. On it rises Romanesque San Giorgio in Velabro, repository of the Latin inscription that once graced the archway.

Cloister and Church of Cosma and Damiano

FORUM
Entrance: Via dei Fori Imperiali 1
Metro: Colosseo
Open daily, 8am—1pm and 3pm—7pm
Tel: 06 699 1540

◆

A few hundred yards from the hive-like Colosseum, hidden between the Forum's Sacred Way and the thundering Via dei Fori Imperiali, lies a little-visited sanctuary dedicated to a pair of brothers, Cosma and Damiano. They were doctor-saints of the early church. Look for the oleanders with blazing pink blossoms, the modern bronze sculpture, a ramp, and an arcaded entrance of marble wedged between an ancient brick building and an ochre-hued one about four centuries old. The complex was knocked together over the millennia from the ruins of the Temple of Divine Romulus and the Library of the Forum of Peace. Once inside you'll know that peace has long had the upper hand. Cyclopean stone blocks in the vestibule mark the spot where the ancient marble map of Rome—Roma Urbis—once hung. Beyond, a fountain with winged horses plays in the middle of a cloister

whose tall walls are a wonderfully Roman shade of pinkish-apricot. The potted palms echo their bigger brethren outside, in the real city. There are frescoes under the cloister's vaults, a handful of benches, and a fine nativity scene that draws crowds at Christmastide.

But the main attraction of this sanctuary lies inside the incense-scented basilica. Here you'll find some of Rome's most splendid, colorful mosaics, from the sixth century, perfectly preserved. Stare up and be dazzled. Cosma and Damiano "are attired in the late Roman dress: violet mantles, in gold stuff, with red embroideries of Oriental barbaric effect," as art historian Franz Theodor Kugler put it in the mid 1800s. Peer over the railing in the apse. Below is the rotunda of the lower church, even older than the mosaics. Its door—nearly always shut—gives directly on the Sacred Way. Beneath the rotunda is a crypt older still. The timelessness is tangible.

Via di San Bonaventura al Palatino

PALATINE

Entrances: Via di San Bonaventura 7, Via Sacra
Metro: Colosseo
Open daily

✦

Galled by the entrance fees and tired of the crowds in the Forum and atop the Palatine? The good news is, the Sacred Way also leads *out* of the complex to a quiet corner hardly anyone knows.

Just a few feet beyond the Arch of Titus and the Forum's rear gateway, on the road to the Colosseum, a narrow lane on the right doubles back and climbs to the convent of San Bonaventura al Palatino. Ignore the improvised sign in ungrammatical English telling you to stay out—this is a public thoroughfare. As you mount—gently at first, then steeply—pause every few steps and turn around for the views. Breathtaking? Below you stretch not only the monument-studded Forum and the olive-stippled, green flanks of the Palatine. You'll also see the Colosseum and Capitoline, the Arch of Constantine and the Celian Hill, plus bell towers, columns and cupolas galore. In fact the panorama from this unsung, dead-end street may just rate among Rome's most stunning, partly because it's so unexpected.

As you climb higher, peer through the bars of disused

gates and doorways for keyhole views, and enjoy the growing silence. By the time you've reached the top of the rise, and find the Stations of the Cross, you'll understand why the followers of the Blessed Bonaventura of Barcelona, alias "the Seraphic Doctor," chose this site during the hurly-burly of the Seicento. The humble friary and church were founded in 1625, atop an ancient cistern that once gathered the waters of the Claudian aqueduct. Its ruins slink away, across the cityscape. Painted that peculiar peachy hue so typical of Rome, the vaulting of the homey little church echoes that of the grand, collapsed Basilica of Maxentius below. Bonaventura's relics are under the altar on the left. Don't expect to see droves of worshippers or busloads of tourists. The saint's refuge is blessed indeed.

VILLA BORGHESE

—❦—

Tempietto di Diana and Il Laghetto

VILLA BORGHESE

Entrances: Viale Esculapio, Piazzale Paolina Borghese, Viale del Lago, Viale Pietro Canonica,
Viale dei Pupazzi, Viale Goethe
Metro: Flaminio-Piazza del Popolo, Piazza di Spagna
Open daily

◆

Four hundred years ago, the plutocratic Cardinal Scipione Borghese-Caffarelli set out to create a suburban park fit for himself and his glorious family. Borghese was the nephew—*il nipote*—of powerful Pope Paul V. He incarnated nepotism. Little could this blueblood of Tuscan origin imagine that the masterpiece of landscape and garden architecture he envisioned would become not only Rome's most celebrated, but also its most popular public park. Nowadays in the very center of town, Villa Borghese is a democratic refuge where even the descendants of the cardinal's servants can enjoy the cooling shade. Scores of sculptures, fountains, follies and ruins fill the park's two hundred rolling acres, which were embellished over the centuries by the cardinal's heirs. Some of the dark ilexes planted in the 1600s survive. Stroll in their bowered shadows past the perfect oval of Piazza di Siena, the smaller of the park's two horse-racing tracks, framed by venerable umbrella pines. Climb up the slight incline, past the so-called Casina di Raffaello (it's actually a church) to the neoclassical Tempietto di Diana, crowned by a bronze pine cone. Built in the late 1780s, the temple is

a handsome perch from which to observe passersby. Locals sometimes play chess or cards atop the half-column in its center.

A few hundred yards west, beyond the gates on Viale Pietro Canonica, another leafy path leads to a pond and a second neoclassical temple, this one dedicated to Aesculapius. It rises atop a tiny island flanked by a centuries-old oak. Amid the temple's white marble perfection stands the hard-driven, authentically ancient statue of the god of medicine, whose original home was the Tiber Island. Unearthed, restored and set up here in 1785, Aesculapius has been the object of quiet veneration ever since. Flotillas of ducks and geese guard him, vying with the handful of rowboats launched on the lake in fine weather by courageous youngsters. Pick a bench and listen to the waterworks gushing, the waterfowl quacking, and the piratical oarsmen laughing. If that's too noisy, try one of the farther -flung corners of the lake compound, where pungent bay laurels and scented viburnum overhang a serpentine stream. The effect is appropriately medicinal.

Courtyard of Museo Pietro Canonica

—◦◦◦—

VILLA BORGHESE

Entrance: Viale Pietro Canonica 2
Metro: Flaminio-Piazza del Popolo, Piazza di Spagna
Park open daily, museum open Tuesday–Sunday 9am–7pm
Tel: 06 884 2279, 060608, www.museocanonica.it

✦

Near the geographic center of Villa Borghese, across from the elegant equitation track at Piazza di Siena, the rarely visited, pinkish, castellated building called the Fortezzuola houses the Museo Pietro Canonica. Look for the bronze sculpture of a laden mule and a World War One Alpino soldier, enter the archway behind them, and prepare to be entranced. Framing an octagonal wellhead covered by climbing roses is a garden court from the late 1700s so thick with oranges, lemons and boxwood that you can barely see the benches awaiting in the dusky corners. By a clump of fan-like papyrus, water drips from a lion's mouth into a scallop-shaped basin grown thick with moss. The courtyard's frescoes are ghostly, so weathered that you can barely make out the trompe-l'oeil heads.

Surprises await inside the museum, where sculptor Pietro Canonica lived and labored from 1926 to 1959. Never heard of him? Canonica was huge a century ago. Born in Moncalieri in 1869, he made his fortune in Rome by portraying Europe's aristocracy and military heroes. Giant plaster casts stand in vast workshops, marble carvings jut from walls, and the sculptor's tools, personal effects, furniture and collections fill a maze of rooms. This may just be Rome's most atmospheric house-museum, the magic redoubled by solitude: the crowds are definitely elsewhere.

The Pincio

at the **VILLA BORGHESE**

Entrances: Piazza del Popolo, Viale G. D'Annunzio, Viale Trinità dei Monti
Metro: Flaminio-Piazza del Popolo, Piazza di Spagna
Open daily

◆

Everyone knows and cannot help flocking to Piazzale Napoleon I at the Pincio, the hilltop parklands above Piazza del Popolo, fronting the vast Villa Borghese. True, from the piazzale the view of the Janiculum and the Vatican, Santa Maria del Popolo, and the twin churches of Santa Maria dei Miracoli and Santa Maria di Montesanto on the piazza below, pleasantly takes the breath away. Or is it the serpentine staircase you climb to get to the top? Never mind. One cannot help marveling at the emptiness of the rest of the Pincio. Its groomed alleys of ilex and plane trees, punctuated by parterres with palms and umbrella pines, form an urban refuge of the first order. Fountains splash in the sun, an antique water clock ticks in the shadows, and scores of lichen-frosted, sculpted busts stare blankly, commemorating Italy's heroes. Best of all, the prospect from the corner of the park's Viale di Villa Medici, along the edge of the French Academy's grounds, flanking the rococo Casina Valadier, is every bit as lovely as the famous panoramic point of Piazzale Napoleon I. If only everyone knew. On second thought, perhaps it's best to keep quiet about this little secret.

COLOSSEUM, MONTI

Parco di Traiano und Domus Aurea

MONTI, *near the* **COLOSSEUM**
Entrances: Via della Domus Aurea, Via Labicana, Piazza del Colosseo
Metro: Colosseo
Open daily

◆

The Colosseum goes by one name, but the hilly parklands abutting it to the southeast have at least three nowadays: Colle Oppio, Domus Aurea, and Parco di Traiano. That's because the Colle Oppio is the name of the hill; the buried Domus Aurea (the Golden House of Emperor Nero) once sat on it; and Trajan's baths were built on top of the emperor's golden ruins.

Use whatever appellation you prefer, climb the staircases and paths into the hilly park, and enjoy a leisurely stroll amid the palms, flame cypresses, rose garden and towering vestiges of empire. The views are intimate, dominated by the Colosseum, as you might expect. But your eye will also reach beyond to the Palatine, and up and down Via Labicana, site of the splendid Romanesque church of San Clemente.

While you won't want to miss what's left of the subterranean Domus Aurea, including the frescoed "grottoes" famously scarred by the graffiti of Raphael and other genial vandals, you can perfectly well stay above ground, enjoying the sun and fresh air free in the park. There's a landscaped fountain of hewn white stone surrounded by a deep, dark grove of ilex trees (with an old-fashioned snack bar), and many a shady nook where locals come to cool out, read or nap. If you're troubled by the graffiti, remember Raphael, whose 1480s signature, like those of many others since, is still visible below ground.

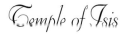

Temple of Isis

MONTI, *near the* **COLOSSEUM**

Entrances: Via Ludovico Muratori, Via Ruggero Bonghi, Via Pasquale Villari, Piazza Iside
Metro: Colosseo
Open daily

◆

How did Isis, daughter of Geb, mother of Horus, make her way from ancient Egypt to the Seven Hills of ancient Rome? A longish volume would be needed to recount the tale. By the Republican era, the cult of Isis, the ideal wife and mother, protector of many things animate and otherwise, had spread throughout the Graeco-Roman world. Several temples to her cropped up in Rome. The first was dubbed Iseum Metellium, and was built by Publius Metellius Pius in 80 BC. Though no one is absolutely sure of the attribution, archaeologists have identified the remains of the glorious, gilt temple in the weathered conglomeration of bricks, tufa and marble flanking a small square, Piazza Iside. It hides some one hundred yards north of Via Labicana, about a quarter mile east of the Domus Aurea, in a charming, hilly, untouristed enclave. Truth be told, if Isis could see her temple today, she might weep. But curious explorers will be intrigued by the strangely wonderful orb-and-conch fountain, a functioning relic from the Fascist era, not to mention the handsome, sweeping staircase, and the imposing apartment buildings and school, all built during the reign of Mussolini, and posed around the supposed temple. A foursome of stripling orange trees is just beginning to cast a beneficent shadow on the benches of the freshly renovated piazza. Given time, they will doubtless grow and spread, as the cult of the goddess did so efficiently.

Via del Colosseo

MONTI, *near the* **COLOSSEUM**
Entrances: Via delle Carine, Via Cavour, Via Frangipane, Piazza del Colosseo
Metro: Colosseo
Open daily

◆

Dodge the plastic-clad gladiators waving wooden swords in front of the Colosseum, or scamper off busy Via dei Fori Imperiali, and take refuge in Via del Colosseo. Nowadays a back road, it was once a main street converging on the colossal amphitheater built by Flavius. Go to numbers 16–19, facing a caper-draped brick wall and rusticated doorway overhung by towering trees and garlands of ivy. You're standing around the corner from a pocket-size Baroque church, its weathered, russet façade forever hemmed by parked cars. This unexpected enclave, cobbled and elevated a yard or so above street level, forms a tiny triangle of bliss, where red bougainvillea and purple wisteria creep across the puckered, peach-hued plaster of centuries-old buildings. A humble Madonna gazes down beatifically at you from a leafy niche, inviting you to sit on the short flight of stairs and rest a spell. Rosemary and sage grow along one side of the triangle, within reach of someone's kitchen window. This is pure Rome. Sure, a high school and grammar school face each other down nearby Via delle Carine, but the yelps of students fade into the background hum. Lift your eyes. Above the tiled rooftops you'll glimpse the battered last tier of the Colosseum one long block to the southeast, a million miles away when measured in terms of atmosphere.

Via del Colle Oppio

MONTI, *near the* **COLOSSEUM**

Entrances: Via del Colle Oppio, Via del Fagutale, Via delle Terme di Tito, Via della Polveriera
Metro: Colosseo
Open daily

◆

Talk about a bench with a view: colossal stonework, a piazza swirling with traffic, the Forum, and the pine-studded Palatine lie directly before you. It's a mystery how the countless millions who throng the Colosseum can miss this solitary, stone bench on a hillock no more than a hundred yards as the raven flies from the city's most famous monument. One reason is straightforward: the lower entrance is always locked. Don't be discouraged. From the Colosseum subway station walk up the steep, curving staircase, cross Via Nicola Salvi and continue up the slight incline following the right-hand sidewalk on Via del Fagutale. Turn right at the first street—Via del Colle Oppio.

This hill was once covered in its entirety by the Domus Aurea—Nero's Golden House. Were it still standing today, the Colossus—the 120-foot bronze statue for which the Colosseum is named—would have risen to your right, putting you eye to eye with the man who fancied himself the sun god, and probably set Rome on fire to make room for his mansion and grounds. Luckily, the Venerable Bede, writing in the early 700s AD, got it wrong when he predicted that "as long as the Colossus stands, so shall Rome; when the Colossus falls, Rome shall fall; when Rome falls, so falls the world." Shortly after Bede fell, the Colossus was melted down and reused, in the best tradition of the Romans and their barbarian heirs. For the time being, the Colosseum stands, and so do Rome and the world. You can sit here for hours undisturbed, contemplating eternity.

Villa Aldobrandini

≈◦◦◦≈

MONTI, *near the* **COLOSSEUM**
Entrance: Via Mazzarino 11
Metro: Cavour, Repubblica, Barberini
Open daily, sunrise to sunset

◆

Imagine a Roman hilltop 1,900 years ago covered by warehouses full of the goods sold at Trajan's Market, a busy shopping arcade and tower complex across the street and downhill from where you're standing. Now fast forward into the 1500s, when the Dukes of Urbino build a stately Renaissance villa atop the crumbled warehouses, and landscape the hillside into a charming panoramic garden wrapped in high walls. Tuneful fountains splash and towering trees shade gravel lanes, lawns and handsome corner pavilions. The intimate, insider's view takes in Trajan's complex, the presidential palace—il Quirinale—and much of central Rome, dome to

glistening dome. In the late sixteenth century the Aldobrandini clan take over, adding their telltale ornaments—a six-pointed star and massive cannonballs.

Back to the twenty first century: miraculously, the villa and park not only survive, they thrive, hidden on three sides by steep, caper-shagged embankments thirty feet tall. Perched above Piazza Magnanapoli, at the start of broad Via Nazionale, Villa Aldobrandini must be Rome's best-kept-

secret park. The family's former residence on abutting Via Panisperna is off-limits, but a wrought iron gate on a side street, Via Mazzarino, leads to a zigzag staircase that mounts the ancient ruins, past a headless statue in a niche, up to the park's top tier. Cypresses and bay laurels give way to parterres planted with giant ficuses, magnolias, pines, palms, sycamores, camellias and ornamental orange trees. Pick a bench. You can't help feeling airborne. The third-story windows on Via Nazionale stare back at you. On the opposite side of the park, you can practically reach out and touch the porch of SS. Domenico e Sisto. Santa Caterina a Magnanapoli and Trajan's Market spread below. Are the park's Renaissance and rococo sculptures posted there to keep guests company? Maybe. It certainly feels like no one but the gardener has set foot here in a hundred years.

CELIAN HILL, SAN GIOVANNI, THE LATERAN

—◦◦◦—

Oratorio di Santa Barbara

CELIAN HILL

Entrance: Piazza di San Gregorio Magno 2
Metro: Circo Massimo
Open weekends, Tuesday and Thursday 9:30am to 12:30pm
Tel: 06 704 94966

◆

On the far side of the Palatine and Colosseum, Clivo di Scauro is a narrow, steep street famed for its seven flying buttresses and ancient Roman houses preserved beneath the church of San Giovanni e Paolo on the Celian Hill. The site draws increasing numbers of visitors to this otherwise uncrowded neighborhood. Few seem to notice the raised, walled orchard, vineyard and church compound across the way from the Roman houses. Rising here atop a long flight of steps (with a lovely view of the Palatine) is the hill's other prominent church, dedicated to Saint Gregory the Great. To the left of the main staircase, through a gate, behind the walls and fences of the piazza and *divo*, are three small oratories. Underneath them lie Roman ruins.

To reach the oratories, enter the gate and walk up the shady lane through a miniature park under pines, cypresses, spruces and palms. Below, toward the *divo*, lie the orchard and vineyard. Ahead, a loggia flanks Santa Barbara at the end of the lane. Much of the structure, stuccoed in apricot hues, with tidy white trim, dates from the early 1600s. Inside are faded frescoes. A sculpted marble dining table from the third century recalls the riotous days when ancient taverns sited here served food and wine. The guests leaned on *triclinium* couches to quaff and feast. That is why Santa Barbara's oratory, so silent and lonely today, also bears another name: Oratorio del Triclinium.

Villa Celimontana and Villa Mattei

CELIAN HILL

Entrances: Clivo di Scauro, Piazza SS. Giovanni e Paolo, Via della Navicella
Metro: Circo Massimo
Open daily, sunrise to sunset

◆

Half a mile east of the Colosseum, on the ancient Roman road fronting the round basilica of Santo Stefano Rotondo, the ship-shaped Navicella fountain splashes merrily, signaling you to halt. Another famous church of the third or fourth century, Santa Maria in Domnica (aka Santa Maria alla Navicella), faces the fountain. Its distinctive Renaissance portico was added by Sansovino, and beckons to passersby. Why is it that no one seems to notice the arching entranceway to the left? Beyond it lies Villa Celimontana, among Rome's loveliest but least known parks. Could it be that the plaque on the gateway discourages visitors? Headquartered here in handsome Villa Mattei is Italy's national geographical institution. No matter. The public is welcome.

Formal parterres with boxwoods, sculptures and gravel lanes lead to a series of shady groves splayed across the hilltop. The usual Roman extravaganza of umbrella pines, palms, cedars, bay laurel and ilex is made even more alluring by a knee-high forest of acanthus, seemingly scattered here to match the curling decorations distinguishing

95

the Corinthian capitals, whose designers were inspired by this plant. Ancient tombstones, sections of fluted column, and Renaissance fountains, including the mossy Fontana del Fiume, add to the charm. These seem positively recent when compared to the park's most venerable object: in a copse of trees on the south side is an obelisk from Heliopolis, carved in the thirteenth century BC, hauled to Rome two thousand years ago and erected on the property in the 1570s by Giacomo Mattei. He transformed the area from vineyards and orchards into a private paradise. After umpteen vicissitudes, in 1813 Manuel Godoy y Alvàrez de Faria, minister of Carlos IV of Spain, took over. His honorary title was "Prince of Peace." Quietude is still the specialty. Within the park stands an isolated chapel; below is Rome's municipal plant nursery and experimental agricultural station; beyond it is another, smaller, humbler park, accessible from a driveway flanking the church of San Gregorio Magno.

Museo Storico della Fanteria and Museo Storico dei Granatieri

———∞∞———

THE LATERAN

Entrances: Piazza Santa Croce in Gerusalemme 7–9, Via Eleniana

Metro: Porta Maggiore

Open: Infantry and musical instrument museums open weekdays 9am to 1pm (noon on Friday);
Grenadiers museum open Tuesday, Thursday, Saturday 10am to noon

Tel: 06 702 7971, 06 702 8287

✦

Whether or not weapons, uniforms, flags and fading documents, or musical instruments are your thing, you will not want to miss the gardens of this museum complex, dedicated to the deeds and memory of Italy's courageous infantrymen and grenadiers, from the Risorgimento onward. Its two buildings are separated by a landscaped park. Stroll around the gravel paths of the pocket-sized green area fronting the weathered former barracks building on Via Eleniana, under magnolias, cypresses and scented pittosporum shrubs. The view of the Baroque façade of the Basilica of Santa Croce in Gerusalemme is sublime.

Behind this building is a slightly bigger park remarkable for its lonely aspect. The grass grows high, but never high enough to mask the palm trees and soaring spruces, the pair of World War Two tanks, or the equestrian sculpture of Victor Emmanuel II, united Italy's first king. For a backdrop the mounted king boasts the imposing brick ruins of the Domus Sessoriano, the presumed residence of Emperor Constantine the Great. If you're an intrepid explorer, follow the driveway between the museum and the basilica, jog left and enter the archeological park where excavations are underway. A vast field and range of giant sycamores gives the spot a rustic, rural feel.

THE AVENTINE, PICCOLO AVENTINO, OSTIENSE, GARBATELLA

Clivo di Rocca Savella, Parco Savello, Giardino degli Aranci

THE AVENTINE

Entrances: Via di Santa Sabina, Lungotevere Aventino
Metro: Circo Massimo, Piramide
Park open daily, 7am to 7pm; Clivo di Rocca Savella open sunrise to sunset

◆

The first sweet-orange tree ever planted in Rome grew for seven centuries atop the elegant Aventine Hill, in a courtyard flanking the medieval church of Santa Sabina. Today, on the opposite side of the church, the panoramic Parco degli Aranci, site of the Rocca Savella fortress, best known nowadays for its view of the Vatican, is stippled by scores of orange trees. The scent of their blossoms, and the shade they cast over the carefully tended, daisy-dotted lawns and convenient benches provides a welcome respite from Rome's abundant sunshine.

A drinking fountain splashes in the middle of the park and rows of pines rise like green parasols. From the panoramic parapet suspended above the Tiber-side avenue, the Parco degli Aranci affords the best possible prospect not only of Saint Peter's dome, but also Santa Sabina—the perfect perch for lovebirds.

Linking the park to Lungotevere Aventino along the Tiber is a sloping alley, Clivo di Rocca Savella. Car-free, mossy and picturesquely weed-grown, the *clivo* is as atmospheric as it is empty. Stray cats own it. At night, the iron gates are shut though rarely locked. If you feel you've entered a moat, you're right: in the Middle Ages, the Aventine was a citadel, Rocca Savella its main fortress. The alley follows its walls. A rusticated archway marks where a drawbridge used to be. The Savelli clan built the fortress before the year 1000 and they held court here, safe from Vatican intrigue. Far from being a dungeon, nowadays the Aventine is among Rome's most sought-after neighborhoods. It provides lucky residents with that greatest of contemporary luxuries: peace and quiet.

Roseto Comunale (Rose Garden)

THE AVENTINE

Entrance: Via di Valle Murcia
Metro: Circo Massimo
Park open daily, 9am to 7:30pm from mid-May to mid-June only
Tel: 06 574 6810, www.comune.roma.it

◆

Not all flowers fade fast. Sniff the air as you wander around the Circus Maximus, searching for memories of chariot races. You might pick up the scent of Rome's eternal rose garden. Its 1,100 varieties of rose brighten and perfume a slope sculpted from the edge of the Aventine, immediately above the elongated oval of the ancient circus. Climbing roses creep into the flame cypresses on the garden's edge. Red roses, pink roses, yellow, white and even green roses sprout and spill from all sides. Rome's gorgeous rose garden may be small by global standards, but the views it affords of the Palatine are stupendous, and its roots run deep, even though it was opened as recently as 1950. Back in the third century BC, the site was given over to sumptuous floral displays, and the wild celebration of fertility: the Temple of Flora stood here. Greenery remained the theme even when the slope became the official orchards and cemetery of Rome's Jewish community, from the mid-1600s until the cemetery moved in 1934 to Rome's monumental burial ground, Campo Verano. The sacredness of the spot explains the Jewish memorial set up near the entrance and the shape of the garden's south-side amphitheater, whose seven alleys evoke a menorah. On the garden's north side are twin gazebos. Even when the garden is closed—eleven months of the year—you can walk between the north and south sections on car-free, pine-lined Via di Valle Murcia. Perch on the main staircase and drink in the atmosphere.

San Saba

PICCOLO AVENTINO

Entrances: Via di San Saba 22, Piazza Gian Lorenzo Bernini 20
Metro: Circo Massimo
Open weekdays 8am to noon and 4 to 7:10pm, weekends 9am to 1pm and 4 to 7:30pm
Tel: 06 645 80140, www.sansaba.it

◆

Some foreign chroniclers churlishly call this surprising knoll south of Viale Aventino the "Pseudo-Aventine," while others prefer "poor-man's Aventine." The Romans are kinder, using the diminutive *piccolo*—little, or lesser Aventine. Whatever the name, the charm of San Saba and its surroundings is great. A walled forecourt of brick masks the church from passersby on curving Via di San Saba. Flanked by shade trees, a short staircase leads to a threshold of marble worn by pilgrims's feet. Beyond it lie the grassy church court and the portico of this paleo-Christian site built against the ancient Aurelian Walls. Stacked atop each other or fitted into the walls are parts of sarcophagi and stonework unearthed here during restorations: San Saba has seen much in its 1,300 years. Before you enter the church, pause long enough to admire the carved knight with a falcon poised delicately on his hand, and travel back in time. How reassuring it is to know that before they were sainted and magnified beyond human proportion, the matronly Sylvia would come here daily, carrying a bowl of hot vegetable soup for her son, later known as Gregory the Great.

Piazza Gian Lorenzo Bernini and Piccolo Aventino

PICCOLO AVENTINO

Entrances: Via di San Saba, Via Bramante, Via Andrea Palladio, Via Salvator Rosa, Via Carlo Maderno
Metro: Circo Massimo, Piramide
Open daily

◆

Girded by the Aurelian Walls southeast of Testaccio, near the Pyramid of Cestius and abutting the Protestant Cemetery, the Piccolo Aventino neighborhood used to be a vineyard attached to the monastery of San Saba. It was from San Saba and the hulking Aurelian Walls that inspiration came to the designers of the district's early low-cost housing units, built just after 1900. Ranged along quiet, narrow, one-way streets and dead ends framing a center-piece park, Piazza Gian Lorenzo Bernini, these are two-story projects that today's modest earners would probably dream of occupying. Constructed from sturdy, simple yet handsome brickwork, each has a pocket-sized garden. Branches laden with oranges or blue plumbago blossoms hang over the sidewalks. Willows weep, palms and pines rise over the roofs. Landscaped stairways lead from this elevated enclave to Viale Giotto and Piazza Albania, the main roads encircling it from below. Not only is the Piccolo Aventino serene and pleasant to behold, its streets are ennobled by the names of great architects and artists, many of them bitter rivals in their day. As to whether the preternaturally proud Bernini, Palladio, Rosa and Bramante, the visionary Alberti, the divine Giotto or the tormented Borromini would approve of the *piccolo* in the name, or their proximity to each other on the map, is a question worth asking.

Piazza dei Cavalieri di Malta and Piranesi Monument

THE AVENTINE

Entrances: Via di Santa Sabina, Via di Porta Lavernale
Metro: Circo Massimo, Piramide
Open daily

◆

When gazing upon the teetering, ivy-draped romantic ruins of Rome how many times have you heard people exclaim, "It looks like a print by Piranesi!" Probably the most celebrated printmaker of the eighteenth century, Giovanni Battista Piranesi designed few buildings. Only a handful were built. Among them are the church of Santa Maria del Priorato, normally closed to the public and wrapped by the private gardens of the Knights of Malta. He also built the small square facing the Priorato, on the southern end of the Aventine. Adorned with obelisks and encrusted with the trophied war memorials of the mysterious Knights, this curious corner of the city sits atop the celebrated laurel grove of Titus Tatius. He was the Sabine king who ruled Rome alongside Romulus. Long before that, if Virgil is to be believed, the area was the haunt of the smoke-belching giant Cacus, where "the ground was always warm with fresh blood, and the heads of men, insolently nailed to the doors, hung there pallid with sad decay." Nowadays the neighborhood is tidy and safe, guarded 24/7 by Carabinieri; the Knights of Malta, and various embassies, are occupants.

The only disturbance, in fact, comes in the form of curious tourists, lured by the famous view of Saint Peter's dome, framed by the keyhole in Piranesi's doors. The doors seal off the grounds of the Knights' headquarters and are opened only to the pious and powerful—or groups with reservations. The piazza is egalitarian. Flame cypresses and palms rise behind its extravagantly long, L-shaped back wall, erected in 1765 and conveniently lined by benches. On the far side of them spread the gardens of the church of Sant'Anselmo, also open to all comers, whether knight or pawn.

Piazza Benedetto Brin, Quiet Streets and Corner Gardens of Garbatella

---

GARBATELLA

Entrances: Via Ostiense, Circonvalazione Ostiense, Viale Giuliano Imperatore,
Via Cristoforo Colombo, and many others
Metro: Garbatella
Open daily

◆

Deliciously down at the heel and far enough flung to be untouristed, the Garbatella neighborhood on central Rome's southern edge offers contoured streets, quirky rounded squares, curving stairways and leafy courtyards seemingly designed for those who love to stroll or sit and soak up the atmosphere. Umbrella pines rise from backyards, climbing roses or wisteria drape trellises, and sidewalks are groomed into improvised flowerbeds. Historic monuments are few, but endearingly vernacular shrines to the Madonna grace walls at many a turn.

Built from 1920 to the early 1940s, this was Rome's first garden suburb for the working class, a colorful study in eclectic architecture that today looks startlingly postmodern—and would alone be worth a trip out here.

Garbatella spreads across low hills between Via Ostiense and Via Cristoforo Colombo, near the outsized Basilica di San Paolo fuori le mura, and the Catacombs of Commodilla. Pilgrims have passed through for millennia. The neighborhood's name supposedly derives from that of a friendly innkeeper. The welcoming tradition continues. In fact a good place to start your visit is Piazza Benedetto Brin, where the longtime trattoria Dar Moschino seems lifted from a film by Fellini. An arched passageway leads from the trattoria's sidewalk terrace to the first of many hidden courts, which often double as outdoor living rooms and kitchens. Flotillas of laundry flutter from a hundred frumpy buildings, many painted in flaking shades of pink or red: Garbatella is a proud bastion of the left. But today the hammer-and-sickle graffiti, and the aerosol art proclaiming workers' rights, often decorate distinctly upscale haunts. Increasingly gentrified and hip, you're more likely to encounter TV journalists, IT gurus and fashion designers in their Garbatella gardens than the factory workers the place was built to house.

IMP·CAESAR·
VESPASIANVS·
AVGPONT·MAX·
TRIBPOT·VII·IMP·XIV·PP·
CENSORCOSVIDESIGVII·
T·CAESARAVGF·
VESPASIANVSIMPVI·
PONTTRIBPOTIVCENSOR·
COSIVDESIGV·
AVGTISPR·FINIBVS·

POMERIVM·AMPLIAVERVNT·
TERMINAVERVNTQVE·

CIPPO DEL POMERIO VPBANO
POSTO NELL'ANNO LXXV
RINVENVTO QVI LI IP
NEL MCM

TRASTEVERE

Street Corner Shrines and Sidewalk Gardens

―――⟪∿∿⟫―――

TRASTEVERE

Entrances: Vicolo del Cedro, Vicolo del Leopardo, Via della Scala, Via del Mattonato and others
Metro: n/a
Open daily

◆

To the ancients, the Trastevere neighborhood, on the west side of the Tiber, was Trans Tiberim, a not-so-great address. For one thing, the Etruscans lurked just over the hills; for another, much of the quarter wasn't protected until the Christian Era by Rome's city walls. Add to this the fact that Trastevere welcomed foreigners of all kinds, and was the port of impoverished, pungently perfumed Tiber fishermen, and you get the picture: no emperor would be tempted to build a palace here, though a few did develop suburban gardens. They're long gone. The Middle Ages were no kinder, but it's to them that Trastevere owes its inimitable atmosphere: this is central Rome's spunky, funky quarter.

It was in the dark days of old that a tangle of alleys grew between the riverside and the flanks of the Janiculum Hill, wrapping themselves like tendrils around crumbling ruins, leaky aqueducts and a score of tumbledown medieval churches. By adding and subtracting over the centuries, the tangle has become a labyrinth of alleyways, zigzag staircases, cavernous passageways and piazzas the size of a handkerchief. Restaurants, trattorias, cafés, hole-in-the-wall shops, hardware and houseware stores, ice cream parlors and nightclubs spring from all sides like wallflowers. Getting lost in Trastevere is part of the charm of a visit.

Perhaps because there are few parks in the neighborhood, the alleys of Trastevere are a continuous living room–cum–public garden. Houseplants and dwarf cypresses, succulents, bougainvilleas and luxuriant weeds ornament kinks and twists in the cityscape. One particularly well-loved street-corner garden has an improvised shrine—to the Madonna. You'll find it—if you *can* find it—where the dog's leg of Vicolo del Cedro meets another alleyway called Vicolo del Leopardo, in the vicinity of Via del Mattonato, not that you're likely to find *it*, either.

A hundred or so yards east, around the corner of Vicolo del Cedro and Via della Scala, head south in the direction of Piazza di Sant'Egidio. If you're lucky, and if you arrive in the morning, the daily delivery of fresh flowers to a nearby florist's shop may brighten the already colorful street scenery. In any case you will want to arrive in the morning, unless you're joining the shabby-chic party crowd that turns this neighborhood, so peaceful by day, into a stage for wild bacchanalia by night. On the narrow end of Via della Scala, you'll see another humble shrine on the wall before you. This one has a frame and hood, and was erected by parishioners centuries ago, when Trastevere was the hardworking haunt of the authentically poor and pious.

Santa Cecilia in Trastevere

TRASTEVERE
Entrance: Piazza Santa Cecilia 2, Piazza dei Mercanti
Metro: n/a
Open daily, 9:30am to 12:30pm and 4 to 6:30pm
Tel: 06 589 9289

◆

You may well hear divine music as you meditate in the many-layered church of Santa Cecilia in Trastevere, a magical refuge tucked behind high walls and a courtyard on the south side of the neighborhood. But don't confuse this ancient repository, built atop the house from the second or third century AD where the virgin saint lived and is entombed, with the famous orchestra named after her, l'Accademia Nazionale di Santa Cecilia. Its headquarters are across town.

Patroness of church music, Wordsworth's "rapt Cecilia, seraph-haunted queen of harmony" underwent a double martyrdom around AD 250. She first survived a murderous braising in the family steam-bath, and was then partly beheaded with an ax. Somehow she survived that, too, dying later from blood loss. Given this gruesome backdrop, it's a relief to discover once you enter her compound that Cecilia indeed rests in peace. Those who wish to, may see her lifelike effigy and tomb sculpted by Stefano Maderno, and visit the archaeological excavations beneath the church. The frescoes, mosaics and statuary, not to mention the palimpsest of architecture, provide enough to contemplate for many hours.

You can also enjoy a moment of inspired quietude in the open air. An ancient, delicately carved urn from the time of Cecilia is the centerpiece of a fountain that squirts tunefully, surrounded by cobbled paths and lawns, and a miniature rose garden. Oleanders, palmettos, yellow jasmines, blue plumbago and blood-red bougainvilleas vibrate to the muted sound of a choir singing within the church. The medieval porch, held aloft by ancient Roman columns, and the walls and entrance portico of the courtyard, harbor tombstones, carved fragments and slabs of marble, and a milestone from the reign of Emperor Vespasian. If, while gazing at it, your nose picks up heavenly scents that vie with the vegetation to perfume the air, don't be surprised: the back door of a bakery opens onto the courtyard, reminding visitors of the weakness of the flesh.

Via in Piscinula, Via Titta Scarpetta, Vicolo dell'Atleta

TRASTEVERE

Entrances: Via dei Salumi, Via dei Genovesi, Piazza in Piscinula, Lungotevere degli Anguillara
Metro: n/a
Open daily

✦

The whole of Trastevere is amazing for its labyrinth of medieval alleyways. But the tangled web that weaves itself outwards once you've stepped beyond Piazza in Piscinula is particularly remarkable. In the southwest corner of the piazza stands San Benedetto in Piscinula, a humble church. Peek in as you pass by. The confraternities based here might be meeting, their acolytes dressed in colorful vintage costumes. Benedict sojourned here, it's claimed, unaware the sanctuary would one day bear his name, or that it had been built on the ruins of a Roman bathhouse—a *piscina*.

That bathhouse was fed by Trajan's Aqueduct. Rebuilt, slightly rerouted, and rebaptized in 1612 as the Acqua Paula, it still carries water to Rome. Walk up Via in Piscinula, under a canopy of Boston ivy and grapevines, and look for the half-hidden marble plaque on the ochre corner house. It marks the aqueduct's route. Turn east. A few paces up the alley called Via Titta Scarpetta, ancient marble fragments are

incorporated into the walls. Turn again and look back. Rising above the tiled roofs is the campanile of San Benedetto in Piscinula, reputedly the city's most diminutive. The bronze bell, cast in 1069, may well be the oldest in town. When it peals, the neighbors know it.

Both alleys lead to Via dei Salumi. The salami-makers are no longer, but if you cross the lane and continue south on Vicolo dell'Atleta you'll enter a clearing in the medieval forest that is appetizing in several ways. Even a child can reach out and with arms spread touch the walls on both sides. The "athlete" that gave this cobbled, curving way its name, in 1873, is a marble sculpture that once adorned Agrippa's Baths, a Roman copy of Lysippos' bronze Apoxyomenos. You can see the statue in the Vatican Museums. How exactly it wound up buried in the ancient foundations of a medieval palazzo on Trastevere's narrowest alley is a mystery. The building's ground floor and cellar have long housed a wine-themed restaurant, Spirito Divino. The street's name before Apoxyomenos was unearthed here in the 1860s was Vicolo delle Palme, as in palm trees, a reminder of Jerusalem. They fronted Rome's first synagogue, opened in the eleventh century, when Trastevere was the city's Jewish district. Where the pagans of Rome bathed, and the Jews of old prayed, kids now play. The living layers of history bring magic to what might otherwise look dauntingly dark.

THE JANICULUM, MONTEVERDE, VILLA DORIA PAMPHILI

Mausoleum of the Garibaldini, Roma o Morte

—◦◦◦—

THE JANICULUM
Entrance: Via Garibaldi
Metro: Cipro / Musei Vaticani
Open daily

◆

To the Roman mind, freedom fighter Giuseppe Garibaldi and the Janiculum Hill are inextricably associated. Everywhere you look, Garibaldi looms large. Even the streets and squares recall his name. From Trastevere, Via Garibaldi climbs the hill in landscaped loops, joining the Passeggiata del Gianicolo park to slant up and across to panoramic Piazzale Garibaldi for an astonishing view of "the greatest theater in the world," as Garibaldi himself described Rome. The boulevard bearing the general's name passes plaques distilling memories of Garibaldi, plus statues of Garibaldi, his men, and, farther along the ridge, his heroic warrior-wife Anita, not to mention a curious little Garibaldi Museum inside the San Pancrazio city gate at the hill's summit.

The reason is straightforward: the bloody, decades-long struggle to unite Italy was played out across the Janiculum, the highest hill in central Rome, nowadays the placid site of desirable real estate.

Of all the monuments to Garibaldi and the Garibaldini soldiers who fought and fell in 1848–49, 1860 and 1870, the mausoleum poised halfway up Via Garibaldi, facing the church of San Pietro in Montorio, is the most unexpected. An angular, Mussolini Modern temple of white travertine marble, emblazoned with the words "Rome or Death," gazes across the city Garibaldi helped wrest from the papal grip. Guarded by bronze she-wolves, the mausoleum is filled with the bones of valiant fighters, bones that were trundled from one temporary location to the next for decades, until the Duce, in a paroxysm of propagandistic inspiration, ordered the ossuary built in 1941. The grassy, leafy park that encloses it appears to be free of ghosts. It's haunted day and night by dog-walkers, stargazers and romantic couples. Happily, the views are inspiring and life-enhancing. Few visitors seem to know of the bones or what the site commemorates, a measure of just how unwarlike the locals are these days.

Sant'Onofrio al Gianicolo

THE JANICULUM

Entrances: Piazza di Sant'Onofrio 2, Salita di Sant'Onofrio, Via del Gianicolo, Via Urbano VIII
Metro: Cipro / Musei Vaticani
Open daily, 9am to 1pm
Tel: 06 686 4498

✦

"**S**aint Onofrius was a monk of Thebes," wrote a chronicler of centuries past in *Jameson's Sacred Art*, "who retired to the desert, far from the sight of men, and dwelt there in a cave for sixty years, and during all that time never beheld one human being, or uttered one word of his mother-tongue except in prayer." What the saint would think of the fifteenth-century church and convent named in his honor, hidden high atop a staircase crowning the Janiculum, is unanswerable. The maelstrom of Rome swirls below, and the city's celebrated Bambino Gesù, a children's hospital famed for its ambulance sirens, wraps around the back of this monastic complex.

Strangely, the moment you climb the final flight of steps into the gardens at Sant'Onofrio, suspended some twenty feet above Via del Gianicolo, you might as well be in the desert, in the saint's cave. Framed by two old ilex trees, a fountain shaped like a mushrooming birdbath splashes gently, barely audible. Next to it is the requisite bench. Displayed beyond the brick perimeter wall are the domes, towers and trees of Rome, with the Alban Hills in the distance. Breathtaking? Goethe came here to sit and sigh, paying homage, as was long the fashion, to the tormented mannerist poet Torquato Tasso, who died and was buried in the convent in 1547. In the mid-1800s Chateaubriand bustled in, declaring with Romantic fervor that he longed to die in this magical spot, and rhapsodizing over the "genius and glory of unhappiness."

Both these illustrious literati are themselves memorialized by stone plaques on the church, facing the panoramic garden. Ironically, thanks to *The Sorrows of Young Werther* and Chateaubriand steak (sauced with white wine and shallots), the pair have eclipsed their mentor: few people other than Italian scholars read Tasso's twisted verse. Fewer still know who Saint Onofrius was. Luckily you don't need to be a hermit or scholar, or worship melancholy, to enjoy the view and the mossy atmosphere. Once you've soaked it up outside, don't overlook Onofrius' church: the frescoes under the loggia (depicting the life of Saint Jerome) are by Il Domenichino, and the apse boasts works by Baldassare Peruzzi and Pinturicchio. Even more important, make time to tiptoe into the two-tiered cloister. Tasso, Goethe, Chateaubriand and thousands of lesser literary pilgrims have rested in it. So should you, seeking out a bench among the potted ferns and ficuses, a lovely place to meditate—or finally crack open that tome by Tasso you've been meaning to read.

Cloister of the Hotel Donna Camilla Savelli

THE JANICULUM
Entrance: Via Garibaldi 27
Metro: n/a
Open daily
Tel: 06 588 861, www.hoteldonnacamillasavelli.com

✦

On the face of it, cloisters, convents and Francesco Borromini, the seventeenth-century Baroque architect, arch-enemy of Bernini and notoriously beset by gloom, do not normally evoke luxe, calm and voluptuousness. It is precisely these ingredients that come together in the Donna Camilla Savelli, a hotel in the lavishly reconverted Santa Maria dei Sette Dolori monastic complex. You can overnight and enjoy this four-star hostelry hidden at the base of the Janiculum, edging Trastevere. But anyone may enter, not just paying guests. Don't be put off by the stern forecourt. It showcases Borromini's trademark passion for convexes and concaves in unadorned brick. Beyond the foyer and reception area, the main courtyard, once a cloister, is now a welcoming garden café surrounded by the hotel's historic, blush-pink buildings. Guests and visitors may stroll through or take tea and nibble crumpets—or other potables and edibles. A centerpiece fountain shaped like a cloverleaf gurgles, hesitant, it seems, to break the spell. Camellias, climbing red roses and a magnificent scented magnolia lend vertical touches of color, while the rosemary and sage are tucked into tidy beds among terra cotta urns in the courtyard's sunniest spots. A vow of silence is no longer required for admission, but don't be surprised if you find yourself whispering while in this heavenly spot.

Tempietto di Bramante and San Pietro in Montorio

THE JANICULUM

Entrances: Via Garibaldi, Salita di San Pietro in Montorio, Piazza di San Pietro in Montorio 2
Metro: Cipro/Musei Vaticani
Open weekdays 8:30am to noon and 3 to 4pm
Tel: 06 581 3940, 06 581 2806, www.sanpietroinmontorio.it

◆

Perfect proportions, symmetry, balance and harmony are what the Tempietto di Bramante incarnates in stone. Rising in the center of the cloister of the church of San Pietro in Montorio, Bramante's miniature temple is a marvel, with sixteen Tuscan Doric columns and a ribbed dome topped by a lantern. This Renaissance icon has inspired countless architects the world round since it was built in 1504. It marks the point where, some believe, Saint Peter was crucified, his body hung upside-down as a sign of humility. Other, older legends claim that the Janiculum's Montorio outcrop was the rock upon which Noah's Ark came to rest when the floodwaters subsided. Those of a scientific bent point out that "Montorio" is none other than the ancients' "Mons Aureus," a golden mount composed of yellowish clay. Whatever your belief, there is unquestionably something divinely peaceful about this place—especially when the wedding parties are absent: this is probably the most popular spot in Rome for brides and grooms to be photographed. Get the full effect of the mountain's magic by climbing the Via Garibaldi uphill from the Porta Settimiana city gate in Trastevere, curving left, then right, up the flight of sweeping steps called Salita di San Pietro in Montorio. It's lined by Stations of the Cross. At the summit, towered over by long-necked palms, the wide, white façade of the church awaits. Pause, inhale deeply and survey the view before you enter the cloister. Its beauty takes the breath away.

Passeggiata del Gianicolo, Villa Aurelia, Aurelian Walls

THE JANICULUM

Entrances: Via Garibaldi, Via del Gianicolo, Via Urbano VIII, Salita di Sant'Onofrio
Metro: Cipro/Musei Vaticani
Open daily

✦

The Janiculum may not be one of Rome's original Seven Hills, but it is the highest and fairest of them all. It also has an impressive pedigree: wrapped by the ancient Aurelian Walls, it's named for a yet-to-be-discovered temple to Janus, or perhaps for the fortified city gate of early Rome designed to keep the Etruscans at bay. Famous for Piazzale Garibaldi and the panoramic, hilltop park called Passeggiata del Gianicolo, you'll find many a tranquil, shady place to stroll or sit here. On the Vatican-end of the esplanade, for instance, there's an open-air amphitheater flanked by the bedraggled remnants of an oak tree, where the poet Torquato Tasso often meditated over four hundred years ago.

Perhaps the most beautiful spot of all is the summit of the Janiculum, crowned by Villa Aurelia, owned by the American Academy in Rome. Unless you're a guest of this prestigious institution, you can't enter its gardens, which boast some of Rome's oldest, tallest pine trees. But you can do pretty well by seeking out the tiny, triangular, wildflower-strewn park immediately below the villa, abutting the Aurelian Walls. It's easy to miss. A landscaped staircase curls up from the Passeggiata del Gianicolo, a few feet beyond the elaborate iron gateway facing the Fontanone, a monumental fountain. Seen through a screen of sycamores and Judas trees, Rome lies at your feet. The French Academy, at Villa Medici across the Tiber, stands at a satisfyingly lower altitude. As philanthropist Clara Jessup Heyland remarked over a century ago, when she first contemplated giving Villa Aurelia to the American Academy in Rome, "Bonjour France! Some day I hope *America* will greet you from this place!" America does, delightedly, and has since 1910.

Villa Sciarra

MONTEVERDE

Entrances: Via Dandolo, Via Calandrelli, Viale delle Mura Gianicolensi

Metro: n/a

Open daily, 7am to sunset

◆

Decadent, sensual, ripe beyond harvest—such are the word-images summoned in Italian minds when the name Gabriele D'Annunzio is pronounced, especially in conjunction with his 1880s novel *Il Piacere*—pleasure—set in the lush, leafy park known as Villa Sciarra. Enclosed on its west side by the imposing papal walls that run along the crest of Monteverde, Villa Sciarra falls steeply down a land-scaped hillside once part of an imperial garden. Certainly, you can poke around the archaeological excavations, and you can also visit the library of the Institute of Germanic Studies, which is based here. But Villa Sciarra's *dannunziano* charms lie elsewhere—in its riotous roses, blousy scented spirea, overgrown parterres, and evocatively weathered eighteenth-century statuary. Fountains spray, their spouts skewed or broken. Pergolas bend under the weight of century-old, knotted mauve wisterias. Shady paths snake under a forest of flame cypresses, bay laurels, elephantine palms and a hundred other species of tree or shrub planted in the early 1900s when the property belonged to the American diplomat George Wurts and his wife Henrietta. She gifted the villa to the

government of Italy in 1932, and it has been open to the public ever since. You'll never be entirely alone in Villa Sciarra. Even its quietest corners—an arbor abutting the papal walls, a palmetto-fringed lawn fronting the Institute of Germanic Studies—are animated by the amorous young adepts of D'Annunzio, or the suggestive sculptures of satyrs and nymphs that inspired the novelist in the first place.

Pines and a Villa

VILLA DORIA PAMPHILI

Entrances: Via Aurelia Antica, Via di San Pancrazio, Via Vitellia, Via Leone XIII
Metro: Cipro / Musei Vaticani
Open daily, 7am to sunset

♦

Rome's biggest park, Villa Doria Pamphili, covers an astonishing 460 acres, spreading its sinuous paths over wooded or grassy hills on the city's western edge, bordering Monteverde and the Janiculum. Fountains, an ancient aqueduct, a stunning seventeenth-century villa with sweeping staircases, plus a landscaped lake and one of Rome's great life-enhancing pine forests, make this a must for seekers of atmospheric tranquility. Joggers, dog-walkers and habitués show up before dawn, but even on weekends and holidays they rarely overfill the park's vastness. Within it several areas are particularly wonderful.

To find them, from the Porta di San Pancrazio city gate, walk cautiously along the Roman consular highway, Via Aurelia Antica. It's probably Rome's most chaotic, two-lane artery. Enter the park through the rusticated main gateway. Topping the rise, beyond the first copse of gnarled ilex trees, rises a pink triumphal arch from the mid-1800s. You've already traversed millennia of fraught history: long before the plutocratic Doria Pamphili clan took over in the Renaissance, these hills were a stronghold of early Rome's arch enemy, the Etruscans. Countless battles have been fought here, including the 1849 clash between Italian independence hero Giuseppe Garibaldi and papal troops backed by the French, memorialized by the arch.

But strife does not cling to these breezy hills. A playful spirit seems to flow with the drinking fountains on your route. Stick to the ridge, following Emperor Trajan's aqueduct, restored and renamed Acqua Paola: it still brings Lake Bracciano's water to Rome. The gravel lane leads to a second gateway. Turn right and climb the splendid staircase at its end, pausing for a view into the villa's formal gardens, where boxwood shrubs form elaborate brocade patterns. A hundred yards further, a pine grove with giraffe-like trunks harbors isolated benches. Rest your feet, feel the fresh sea breezes, and listen for the elusive green parakeets; hundreds of them have taken up residence in the treetops. "Enchanting" is the right word to describe the setting. The gods of old seem to move in the sowing boughs. Beyond the pines, wrapped by bay laurels and ilex groves, a waterfall spills into the park's lake. Who knows, if you're lucky, Jupiter might swan in, surrounded by ducks or geese.

A River Runs Through It

◆

Rome's havens of greenery are often the vestiges of lands once owned by wealthy aristocrats. For centuries, the Doria Pamphili estate on the city's western edge was so vast and so elaborately contrived, with dozens of fountains, follies, authentic Roman ruins, farmhouses, villas, vineyards, hunting grounds in thick woodland, orchards, daisy-dotted pastures and fields, that a small army of servants, including a fulltime architect, were needed to maintain it. The cost was staggering. The property lived its heyday in the 1600s, when Pamphili pope Innocent X ruled Rome. When modern times arrived in the early 1900s, it's no wonder the family sold off some of their holdings, and signed over the rest—nearly five hundred acres—to the municipality, thereby creating the capital's most spacious public park.

The last hundred years appear to have brought few changes. William Dean Howells in 1908 noted that "it is so far off on its hills that it is safe from the overrunning of city feet." Describing the "the long aisle of ilex," he remarked that "I do not suppose there is a more perfect thing of its kind in the world. The shade under the thick sun-proof roofing of horizontal boughs was practically as old as night." The ilexes still stand, now nearly four hundred years old. Follow their contorted trunks to the park café, enjoy a cappuccino, then cross the footbridge over Via Leone XIII, an express route to the coast. You've entered the western side of the park.

Most visitors don't realize that beyond the thoroughfare the seductive hills, forests and pastures continue, preserving *la campagna romana*—the Roman countryside of old. In a green valley, a looping road lined by ornamental flowering plums joins another unpaved track flanked by a stream and a range of towering sycamores. Dreamy? It gets even better. A quarter mile into the park, perched atop a knoll, is the Casale di Giovio, an Imperial-era mausoleum converted into a farmhouse, with a sculpted low-relief above the door, and a miniature botanic garden out front. Sit under the mulberry trees on Viale Maria Carta at the foot of the farmhouse and garden, and listen to the creek flow by.

CASTEL SANT'ANGELO, PRATI, THE VATICAN

—◦◦◦—

The Banks of the Tiber

———❦———

CASTEL SANT'ANGELO, PRATI

Entrances: all embankment streets that start with "Lungotevere"
Metro: Flaminio
Open daily

✦

Without the Tiber there would be no Rome. The city's hills and valleys were carved eons ago by the river and its tributaries. They brought drinking water to the area's prehistoric inhabitants. Later, the Tiber formed the natural moat that separated the lands of Rome's founders from the enemy Etruscans, delivered Romulus and Remus in a floating basket, and allowed Roma Aeterna to thrive. A short but violent river, the Tiber's yearly floods made the early city's low-lying areas uninhabitable. Even when embankments and harbors were built, flooding fouled them and brought death by water-borne disease. That's why in the late 1800s the picturesque riverine sprawl seen in the prints of old was cleaned up, and the Tiber tamed by stone walls so tall and uncompromising that to this day they form a sinuous gorge in Rome's ancient heart. This has its advantages. For one thing, the noise of the city disappears once you clamber down the many marble-paved staircases, under turn-of-the-century lamps and the dangling branches of giant sycamores, and reach the cobbled quays. Another bonus is the breeze that blows upstream from Ostia on the coast, just ten miles away. The views, too, are appealing, especially those of the Vatican's dome as seen from the eastern bank, upstream from Ponte Sant'Angelo. Last but not least, there are no cars or motor scooters. On the western bank a hiking and biking path runs for mile after curvaceous mile, from the city's northern edge, near Ponte Milvio, downstream past Trastevere.

Castel Sant'Angelo Park (Parco della Mole Adriana)

―∞∞∞―

CASTEL SANT'ANGELO, PRATI

Entrances: Piazza Adriana, Lungotevere Castello, Lungotevere Vaticano
Metro: Lepanto, Flaminio/Piazza del Popolo, Piazza di Spagna
Open daily

✦

Ask Romans for directions to the Parco della Mole Adriana—the park's official name—and they'll shrug. Try "Giardini di Castel Sant'Angelo" instead and you'll be led by the elbow to a green garland on the Tiber's banks. In the center of it rises Emperor Hadrian's Mausoleum, a fearsome hulk of scarred stone completed in AD 139. Atop it Gregory the Great spotted an angel in AD 590, or so it's said. The mausoleum was reconfigured as a fortress and became known as Castel Sant'Angelo to sanctify Gregory's vision. Today, the formerly blood-soaked site, once home to despots and anti-popes, is a popular museum, surrounded by a pleasant park, with many hidden nooks and quiet crannies. Stroll on the pentagonal bastions for a view from on high, under the ilexes and pines planted in the 1930s, or walk down the staircases and ramps to the lower level, where kids play soccer and locals walk their dogs, watched over by flame cypresses and headless statues. You can circle the castle without ever leaving the park or encountering a car. On the Vatican side you'll find the elevated secret passageway of the popes called *Il Passetto*, begun by Leon IV in the 840s but only finished 660 years later by Alexander VI around 1500. This is the Eternal City, after all. Inside the castle an ancient ramp spirals up through the darkness, and dungeons and secret tunnels await innocent visitors. There's also a sunny, panoramic café. From it you can gaze into the oasis below and pick out your favorite shady corner, away from the madding crowd and legions of ghosts.

OUTLYING AREAS

———✦✦✦———

Via Appia Antica

OUTLYING AREA

Entrances: Via delle Terme di Caracalla, Via di Porta San Sebastiano
Metro: Piramide, Circo Massimo, Roma Ostiense
Open daily

✦

Who could forget Peter Ustinov playing the mad Emperor Nero and Robert Taylor cast as Saint Peter in the 1951 Cinecittà blockbuster, *Quo Vadis*? You needn't wear sandals or carry a sword to enjoy the Via Appia Antica—the Appian Way—where this swords-and-sandals saga and many others were filmed. Nicknamed the Queen of Roads, the Appian Way is possibly the most renowned of ancient thoroughfares, built by consul Appius Claudius in 312 BC. A fourteen-foot-wide straightaway, its twin rows of umbrella pines and flame cypresses shade timeworn mausoleums and monuments, leading from the center of Rome to Brindisi on Italy's southern Adriatic coast. The first ten miles have been preserved—truly a miracle—and are flanked by the Caffarella Valley nature reserve and the Park of the Seven Aqueducts. This sprawling greenbelt traversed by hiking trails and bike paths is scattered with authentic ruins, watered by sacred springs, and carpeted by pastures where sheep graze and runners do loops many, many miles long.

Only the cars of local residents brave the rough paving stones of the Appian Way. Most of the scarred, uneven road is car-free

(on Sundays it is entirely). Poppy-clotted fields littered with marble and terra cotta shards stretch endlessly. When Saint Peter tramped by, full of foreboding, the broken arches you see today stood tall and proud, water courses on their backs. The most scenic, serene section lies beyond Porta di San Sebastiano. If you walk out to it, en route visit sixth-century Santa Maria in Tempulo, shoehorned into a garden grotto graced by a flying archway. The Baths of Caracalla rise across from it on the landscaped avenue. A few miles beyond the city gate are the catacombs of San Callisto and San Sebastiano—dead quiet, naturally. By taking bus #118 or #218 halfway out, you'll save your feet for the seemingly never-ending, time-tunnel hike into the Roman *campagna*, where the words of Saint Peter still echo: "Whither goest thou?"

San Giovanni a Porta Latina, Parco degli Scipioni

———✦———

OUTLYING AREA

Entrances: Via di Porta Latina 17, Via di Porta San Sebastiano, Via di San Giovanni a Porta Latina
Metro: Circo Massimo, San Giovanni, Re di Roma
Park open daily, sunrise to 7pm; church open daily, 7:30am to 12:30pm and 3 to 7pm
Tel: 06 774 00032 (church), www.sangiovanniaportalatina.com

◆

Romans love frying food in olive oil, and have since ancient times. The mania for gobbling *carciofi alla giudia*—crisp Jewish-style fried artichokes—probably arrived soon after AD 70, when Emperor Titus sacked the Temple in Jerusalem, repatriating booty, slaves and Jewish customs. It's a curious coincidence that not long after that, in AD 92, Emperor Domitian ordered that Saint John the Evangelist be lowered into a cauldron of boiling oil at a site just inside the Porta Latina, a city gate on Rome's southeastern edge flanking the Aurelian Walls.

Clearly Domitian's cook wasn't up to the task: John survived and was exiled to Patmos. Curiouser still, the unsuccessful fry-up was immortalized only in the fifth century, not by one but by two separate monuments. They stand—much modified—to this day. The first is a chapel erected on the spot of the failed martyrdom, the original building replaced in the 1500s by a strange, octagonal construction attributed to Bramante or Antonio da San Gallo the Younger, with later embellishments by Borromini. Or so some experts claim. Next to the chapel is the Parco degli Scipioni, resting place of the Scipio clan, and temporary refuge to local residents, joggers and travelers, who delight in its shady paths and benches.

Back on Via di Porta Latina, head fifty yards toward the center of Rome, turn right at the first lane, and pause to admire the vernacular wall shrine, clinging caper bush, and small, fluted column embedded nearby. The second monument to Saint John the Evangelist is a full-fledged Romanesque church at the end of this dead-end lane, signaled by the spreading branches of a century-old Lebanon cedar. Benches beneath it offer one of the city's more tranquil places to sit. Vines tangle one wall. The portico of the church displays the requisite precious marble fragments. Ancient architectural graffiti on the main door's threshold contrast with a cosmatesque inlay of green and red porphyry. Fronting it, a medieval wellhead of carved milky marble ornamented with Latin script, with matching marble columns on either side, invites the thirsty to drink. This is no longer advisable, unless understood metaphorically. The sweet, silent atmosphere of this far-flung sanctuary certainly is potable.

Villa Ada Savoia

OUTLYING AREA

Entrances: Via Salaria 267, 273, 275; Via di Ponte Salario, Via di Monte Antenne, Via Panama, Viale della Moschea, Viale Romania
Metro: Campi Sportivi
Open daily

◆

Italy's last royal family, the Savoias, reigned in Rome until 1946, when the nation became a republic and said farewell to its kings. Villa Ada was their humble little private home, surrounded by a pocket-sized park, covering nearly five hundred acres between the ancient salt route, Via Salaria, and the confluence of the Tiber and Anienne rivers, on the capital's eastern edge. Ever since the Savoias left, these hilly, pine-stippled parklands, reduced somewhat by speculation, have been a favorite picnicking, jogging, dog-walking, riding and lounging venue for plebeians and bluebloods alike. You can easily spend hours wandering along the park's streams, through deep, dark woods, around the rowing lake, and atop two surprisingly high hills with keyhole views of the city. Or you can explore the Catacombs of Priscilla that underlie Villa Ada Savoia's eastern edge. Millennia before the regal clan showed up, the Romans and Christians lived, loved and died here. Chilling grottoes and romantic ruins lurk in many a sylvan setting. There are also a dozen outbuildings, among them stables designed for the Queen's pregnant horses, a mock

Gothic tower, a Swiss chalet, faux antique temples and tribunes, a coffee house and several aristocratic villas from the 1700–1800s. You may be forgiven for thinking that local pointillists—the Macchiaioli—have dotted the painterly grounds with daisies. Much of the year they grow in such profusion that Villa Ada Savoia's lawns seem more white than green.

Monte Mario: Park and Overlook Café

OUTLYING AREA

*Entrances: Via Trionfale, Via del Parco Mellini, Via del Parco della Vittoria,
Via Edmondo De Amicis and many others*
Metro: Gemelli, Monte Mario
Open daily

❖

Ecco Roma! So the coachmen of old would shout, stopping their rattling conveyances atop Monte Mario when they first spotted Rome from the Via Trionfale, the ancient pilgrimage route from France to the Vatican. Nowadays, arriving by train, plane or car just isn't the same. But the views from Monte Mario—the highest hill in modern Rome, on the city's northwestern edge—are as wondrous to behold as ever.

You can't help wondering why Monte Mario hasn't been developed inch by panoramic inch, and how nearly four hundred acres of this sun-baked, steep, rugged hillside shagged by broom, scrub oak, myrtle, rock rose, arbutus and bay laurel, became a nature preserve in 1987. The story would be long to tell. And what you really want is to get to the summit and hike the roller-coaster trails.

A good place to start is curvaceous Via del Parco Mellini. It branches off Via Trionfale about one hundred yards south of Piazzale delle Medaglie d'Oro and loops up and up, offering paths through pine woods and picnic grounds. If you can't find the road, ask for the national astrophysics institute—Rome's observatory—or

Lo Zodiaco, the café-restaurant next door to it, in business since the 1950s. From its yucca-dotted panoramic terrace you see the view that Martial saw nearly two thousand years ago, his words now engraved in stone: *Hinc septem dominos videre montis et totam licet aestimare Romam* ("From here see the Seven Hills and delight in the whole of Rome"). A bench below the plaque is there in case you swoon.

Consider the above a teaser. The nature reserve actually lies north, beyond the pine grove. Follow Via del Parco della Vittoria, jog left behind a school, and come out at a tatterdemalion pasture where lean horses graze above the Tiber. From here, a tortuous trail twists through the underbrush into the reserve. Slightly wider gravel trails run on the ridge, past an olive and pine grove. Once you've crossed this section and reached the steep city street called Via Edmondo De Amicis, climb it for two hundred yards and jog right on a dirt trail. At its summit rises an immense, gilded statue of the Madonna. Before returning on your tracks, you may justly exclaim *Ecco Roma!*

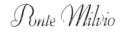

Ponte Milvio

◆

The gory story of Ponte Milvio would soak several unwieldy tomes. Luckily you don't have to be cognizant of the elegant, arcaded bridge's 2,200 years to enjoy a stroll across its smooth, car-free surface above the foaming river. Be warned: you might not be alone, though what you'll probably hear from fellow visitors is sighing and cooing.

Spanning the Tiber on central Rome's northern edge, Ponte Milvio has become a contemporary pilgrimage site for an international cast of lovelorn youth. It featured in the Italian bestselling novel *Ho voglia di te*, a scarlet tale in which young lovers clamp an un-pickable lock to a railing on the bridge. Somehow the fact that this national landmark was recently and expensively restored escaped the novelist's ken. Over the last decade this innocent act of fictional vandalism has inspired droves of real-life couples to lock their own destinies to the parapets. If you didn't bring a lock with you, no worries, itinerant lock-peddlers do a brisk business on site.

History buffs will want to know that Piazzale di Ponte Milvio, on the northern side of the bridge, is where two ancient Roman consular highways met: the Via Flaminia and the Via Cassia. Heavy traffic, floodwaters and vigorous warfare brought down the bridge over and over again. Think of it as a flying patchwork stitched from some of history's great episodes. If most locals irreverently call this hallowed place "Ponte Mollo" it's because *mollo* means waterlogged, a reference, perhaps, to the spongy wooden span built here in the sixth-century AD between the broken pilings of pre-barbarian days. The last devastating battle fought on Ponte Milvio was led by Giuseppe Garibaldi's troops in 1849, when they valiantly failed to free Rome from the proverbial papal yoke. Fortunately no trace of their dynamite remains. Romans use the bridge to cross from the upscale Flaminio neighborhood to the bustling Piazzale di Ponte Milvio market, one of Rome's liveliest, known for what might just be the capital's most flavorful shaved ices and watermelons. A further attraction is the biking and hiking lane on the same bank as the market: it runs downstream clear across central Rome.

Nomentana: Santa Costanza and Sant'Agnese fuori le mura

OUTLYING AREA

Entrances: Via Nomentana 349, Via di Sant'Agnese
Metro: Piazza Bologna
Churches open 9am to noon and 4 to 6pm, closed mornings on Sunday and holidays;
park area open 7am to 10pm daily
Tel: 06 862 05456

◆

This is a magical two-for-one: a round, fourth-century mausoleum-church and an early Romanesque basilica fronted by a forecourt. Both are wrapped by the same small park, complete with ancient ruins, a soccer field, and a neighborhood café, not to mention bocce, basketball and volleyball courts and a sacred grotto. Oh, and catacombs too, in case you feel like going underground. Rest assured, it's worth your time and trouble getting out here (take express bus #36 from Termini train station or #60 from Piazza Venezia).

Silence is golden, and gold abounds in both, but of the two holy places, Santa Costanza is the more famous, for good reason. The joyful paleo-Christian mosaics under the barrel vaults show Dionysian scenes of grape harvesting and crushing, three happy workers in loin cloths gorging on grapes by the bunch. Nearby spread delicate geometric designs, horns of plenty, scallop shells, vases, portrait busts and peacocks, all glowing with gold highlights. An imposing sarcophagus is also carved with a grape-and-wine theme. Funnily Costanza wasn't a saint at all, but Emperor Constantine's daughter; it may have seemed prudent to early churchmen to honor her with the title.

From Costanza's mausoleum walk down the ivy-hung paths, past real, contemporary grape trellises, and find one of the two entrances to Sant'Agnese. The top entrance is a tunnel that slopes down from a portico near the forecourt; the lower entrance is through the façade, unexpectedly turned away from the street. The church, a recent interloper from the seventh century, was built into the catacombs dug out to accommodate the decapitated virgin martyr's remains. They now rest in a silver sarcophagus in this active parish church (Agnes's head is in Sant'Agnese in Agone, in Piazza Navona). A place of pilgrimage, this is one of the city's best-loved shrines. Fronting the lower entrance, shaded by pines and cypresses, several park benches face a grotto crowded with votive plaques and candles, proof of the intensity of many pilgrims' devotion. Close your eyes and you can almost feel it.

Nomentana: Villa Paganini and Villa Torlonia

OUTLYING AREA

Entrances: Via Nomentana 70, Vicolo della Fontana, Largo di Villa Paganini,
Via A. Torlonia, Via Siracusa, Via L. Spallanzani
Metro: Piazza Bologna
Park areas open 7am to sunset daily; museums of Villa Torlonia open 9am to 7pm in spring and summer,
until 4:30pm and 5:30pm in fall and winter, respectively
Tel: 06 0608, www.museivillatorlonia.it

✦

It's a dog's life at Villa Paganini. From the Renaissance to the 1800s, this handsome neighborhood park on Via Nomentana was a rolling green stage facing the architecturally theatrical Casino Nobile—long gone, except a formal gateway. Restored from the grass roots up in 2004, nowadays the grounds are a rambling, romantic landscape of ponds, shady copses, and sunny knolls—with Rome's first official canine playground. Dogs from all walks of life frolic in their own fountain, separated from pushy humans by an iron fence.

Directly across the Via Nomentana is the larger, infinitely more splendid Villa Torlonia, no dogs allowed. Dotted with giant terra cotta urns and monuments, its centerpiece is the colonnaded, splendidly eclectic mansion begun by Giuseppe Valadier in 1802 and completed by the lesser hand of Giovan Battista Caretti in 1840. The villa, park and fanciful structures scattered around it—garden follies, a temple, obelisk, amphitheater, coffee kiosk, chapel and lemon hot house—were restored to the tune of millions and reopened in 2006. Some of Rome's tallest, healthiest palms and umbrella pines thrive here. The landscape rolls gently, with one surprisingly high hillock accessed via a winding path.

Two house-museums are on the grounds, both worth visiting. The Casina delle Civette is a study in the quirky style Italians call "Liberty," a variety of Art Nouveau, with stunning ceramic tiles, crazy roofs, and stained glass. The Casino Nobile instead merges neo-Gothic, neo-Renaissance, neo-Classical and twentieth-century kitsch. Vast ballrooms, lavish dining rooms and glitzy bedrooms display what some call the "Scuola Romana" or "Inter-war Art"—the edgy works produced by Mafai, Cagli, Donghi and others under Fascism. Why here? Villa Torlonia was the residence of Benito Mussolini from 1925 to 1943. The Allied Command took over once the bomb damage had been cleared. Luckily, today, with its extraordinary palms and reflecting pools, Villa Torlonia really is an oasis of quiet, a great place to reflect on the futility of oppression and the healing powers of time.

Index

ABOUT THE AUTHOR

David Downie is an American author and journalist who divides his time between Italy and France; Downie's mother is Roman, and he lived in Rome when young. For the last 25 years he has been writing about European culture, food, wine, and travel for magazines and newspapers worldwide. His books include *Enchanted Liguria: A Celebration of the Culture, Lifestyle and Food of the Italian Riviera*; *Cooking the Roman Way: Authentic Recipes from the Home Cooks and Trattorias of Rome*; *The Irreverent Guide to Amsterdam*; Paris, *Paris: Journey into the City of Light*; and a political thriller, *Paris City of Night*. Downie is the author of three Terroir Guides published by The Little Bookroom: *Food Wine Rome*, *Food Wine Burgundy*, and *Food Wine The Italian Riviera*.

ABOUT THE PHOTOGRAPHER

Alison Harris has worked throughout the world shooting photos for travel books, cookbooks, advertising campaigns, book covers, and magazine articles. She spent much of her childhood in Rome. Her latest books are *Markets of Paris*, *The Patisseries of Paris*, *Chic Shopping Paris*, *Food Wine Italian Riviera & Genoa*, *Food Wine Rome*, and *Food Wine Burgundy*, all published by The Little Bookroom.